Our Pets

Julie Haydon

Contents

Rigby

A Harcourt Achieve Imprint

www.Rigby.com
1-800-531-5015

Our Pets

We have pets.

Pets are lots of fun.

We look after our pets.

Jessica

My Dog

My pet: Buddy the dog

Looks: white and gray

Likes: to go for walks

           to eat his dinner

My job: to fill

           his water **bowl**

Tim

My Cat

My pet: Star the cat

Looks: black

Likes: to play
with her toys

to sleep
on Mom's chair

My job: to brush Star

Simon

My Fish

My pet: Fin the fish

Looks: orange

Likes: to swim
          in the fish tank

          to hide
          in the plants

My job: to feed Fin

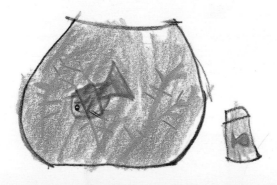

Brianna

My Bird

My pet: Bing the bird

Looks: yellow

Likes: to sing

           to fly in his cage

My job: to fill

           his seed bowl

My Crab

Jayden

My pet: Shelly the crab

Looks: red

Likes: to hide in her shell

        to walk in her tank

My job: to help Mom
        clean her tank

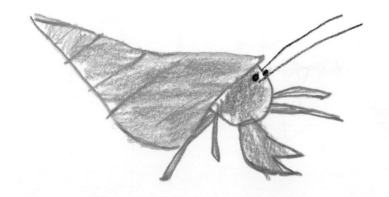

Chris

My Mouse

My pet: Tex the mouse

Looks: white

Likes: to run up my arm

to run on his **wheel**

My job: to play with Tex

to hide him
from our cat

Glossary

bowl

wheel